Francesco
DURANTE
MAGNIFICAT
IN B-FLAT MAJOR
(Formerly attributed to Pergolesi)
Edited by
Clayton Westermann

Vocal Score
Klavierauszug

SERENISSIMA MUSIC, INC.

CONTENTS

1. Magnificat Anima Mea (Chorus) 3

2. Et Misericordia (Soprano, Alto Soli and Chorus) 17

3. Deposuit (Chorus) 21

4. Suscepit Israel (Tenor and Bass Duet) 30

5. Sicut Locutus Est (Chorus) 34

6. Sicut Erat in Principio (Chorus) 38

ORCHESTRA

Bassoon (opt.), Keyboard
Violin I, Violin II, Viola, Violoncello, Double Bass

MAGNIFICAT
1. Magnificat Anima Mea

Francesco Durante
Edited by Clayton Westermann

SERENISSIMA MUSIC, INC.

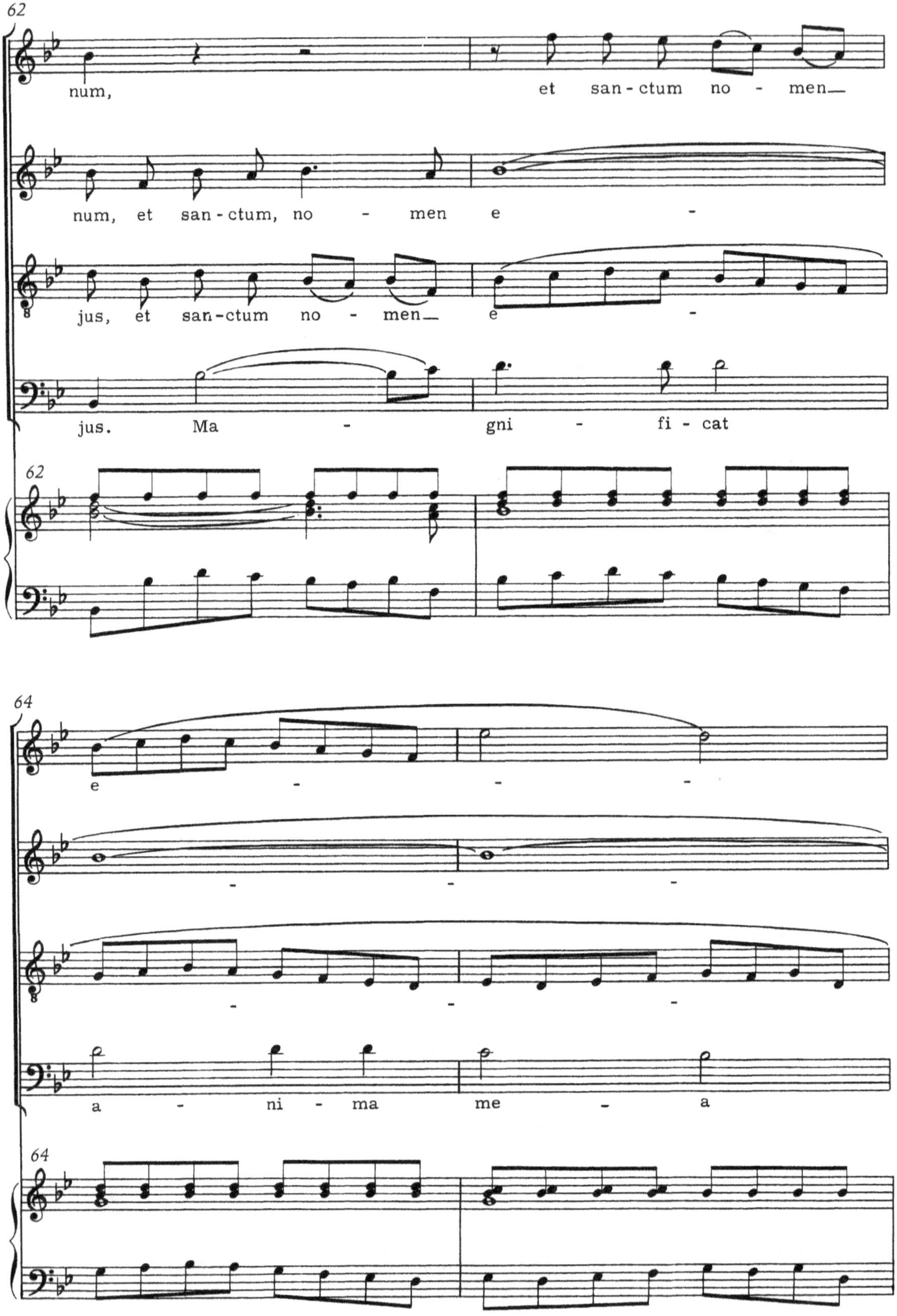
62
num,
et san - ctum no - men
num, et san - ctum, no - men e -
jus, et san - ctum no - men e -
jus. Ma - gni - fi - cat
62
64
e - - -
- - -
- - -
a - ni - ma me - a
64

2. Et Misericordia

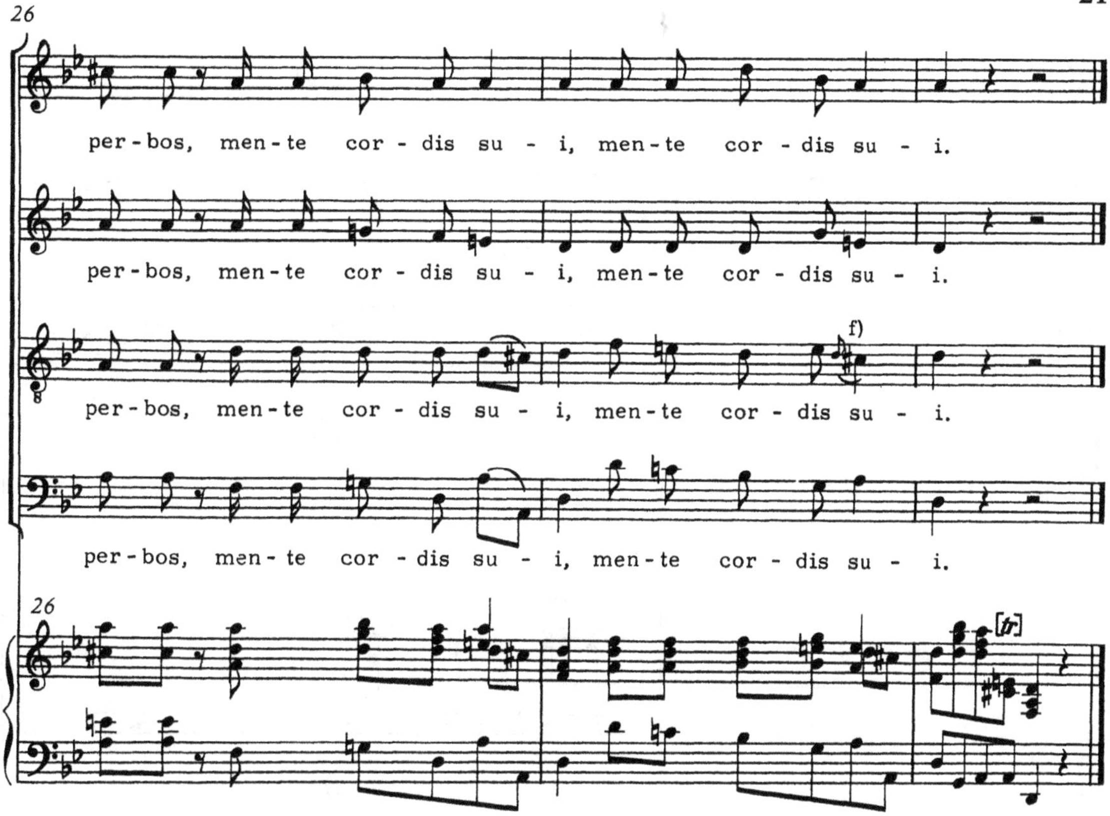
26
per - bos, men - te cor - dis su - i, men - te cor - dis su - i.
per - bos, men - te cor - dis su - i, men - te cor - dis su - i.
f)
per - bos, men - te cor - dis su - i, men - te cor - dis su - i.
per - bos, men - te cor - dis su - i, men - te cor - dis su - i.
26
[tr]

3. Deposuit

[Allegro]
[f]
Alto
De - po - su - it po - ten - tes de se - de, et
Tenor
[f]
Et
[Allegro]
Keyboard
[f]

f)

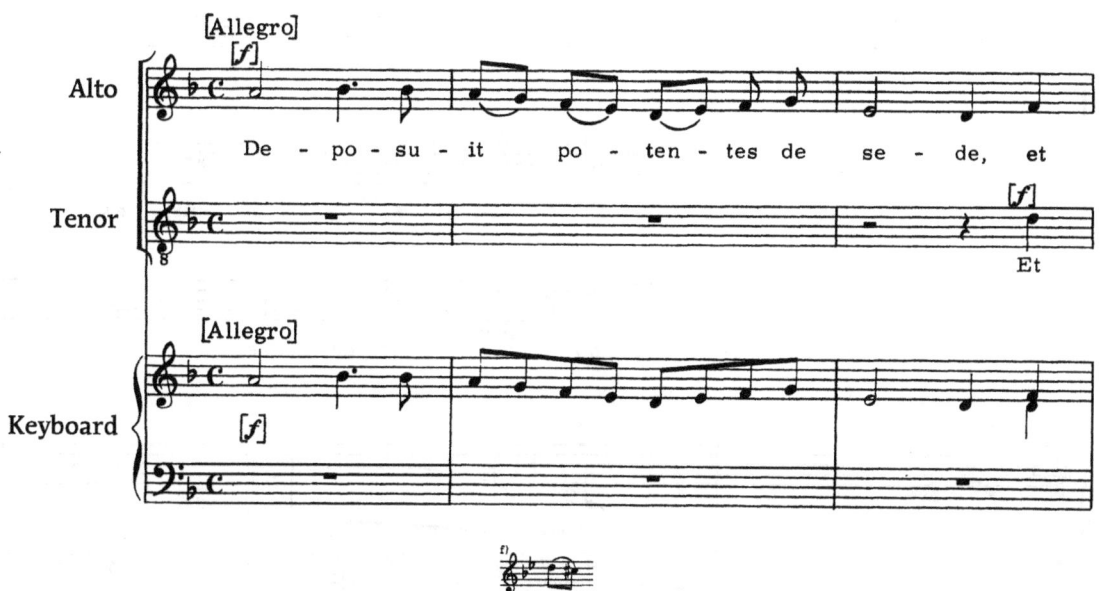

4
(Soprano)
ex - al - ta - - - vit
ex - al - ta - - - vit
(Bass)
4
7
[f]
De -
hu - mi - les,
hu - mi - les, Et ex - al - ta - vit, ex - al -
[f]
De - po - su - it po - ten - tes de se - de
7

10
po - su - it po - ten - tes de se - de, et ex - al -
et ex - al - ta -
ta - vit hu - mi - les,
et ex - al - ta - vit hu - mi - les, et ex - al -
10
13
ta - - - vit hu - mi -
- vit hu - mi - les.
et ex - al - ta - vit hu mi -
ta - - - vit hu - mi -
13

39
a - nes, di - mi - sit in - a - nes, di -
a - nes, di - mi - sit in - a - nes, di -
a - nes, di - mi - sit in - a - nes, di -
- nes, di - mi - sit in - a - nes, di -
39
tr
41
mi - sit in - a - nes, di - mi - sit in -
mi - sit in - a - nes, di - mi - sit in -
mi - sit in - a - nes, di - mi - sit in -
mi - sit in - a - nes, di - mi - sit in -
41

4. Suscepit Israel

5. Sicut Locutus Est

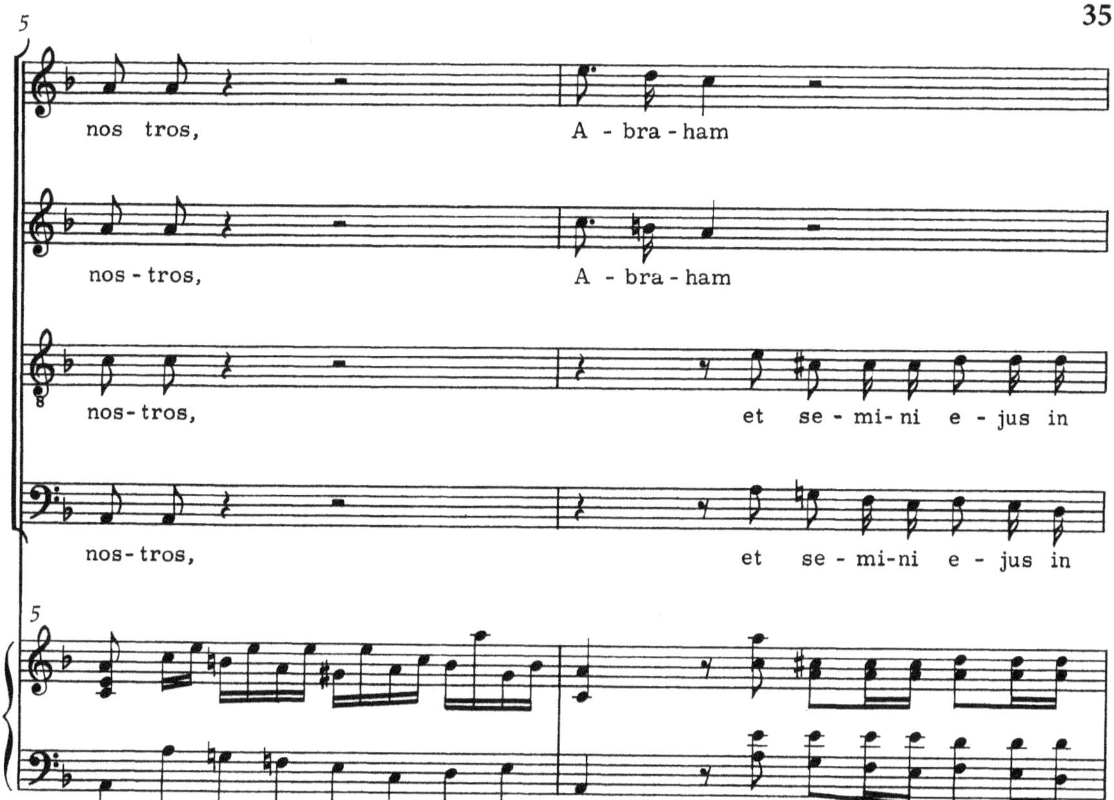
5
nos tros, A - bra - ham
nos - tros, A - bra - ham
nos- tros, et se - mi- ni e - jus in
nos- tros, et se - mi-ni e - jus in
5

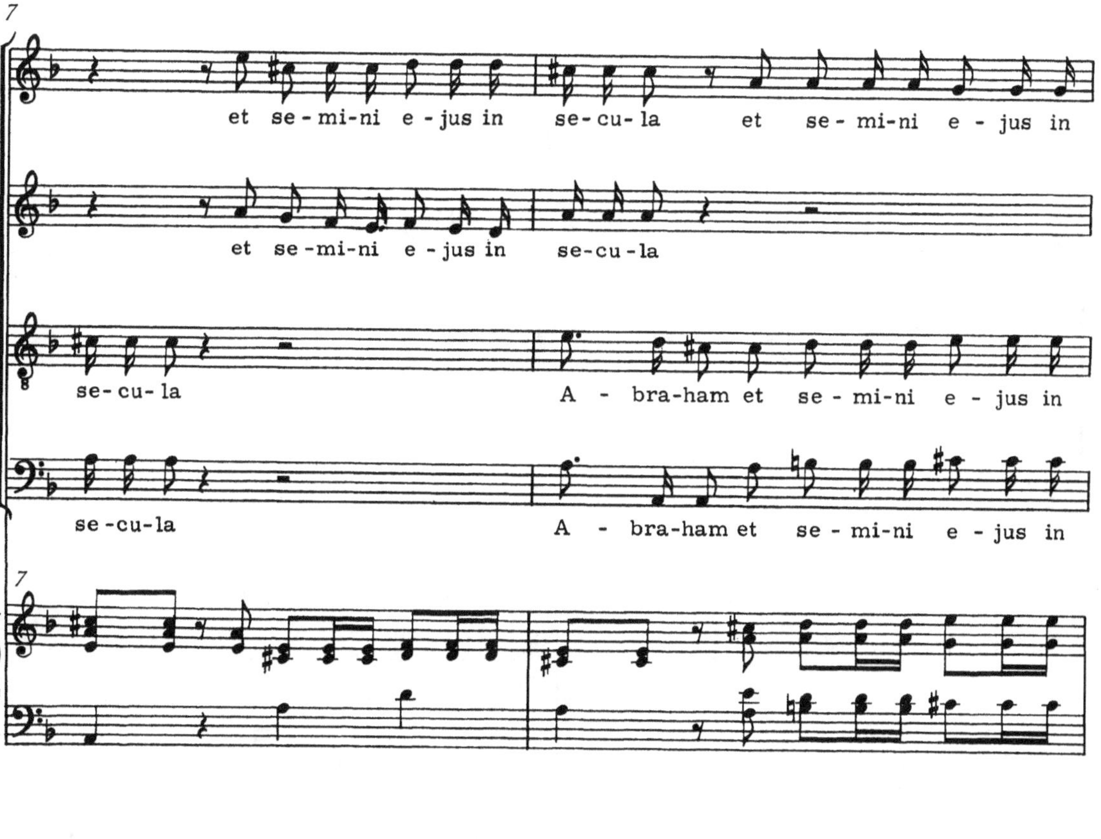
7
et se - mi- ni e - jus in se- cu- la et se - mi- ni e - jus in
et se -mi- ni e - jus in se- cu - la
se- cu- la A - bra-ham et se - mi- ni e - jus in
se -cu- la A - bra-ham et se - mi- ni e - jus in
7

6. Sicut Erat in Principio

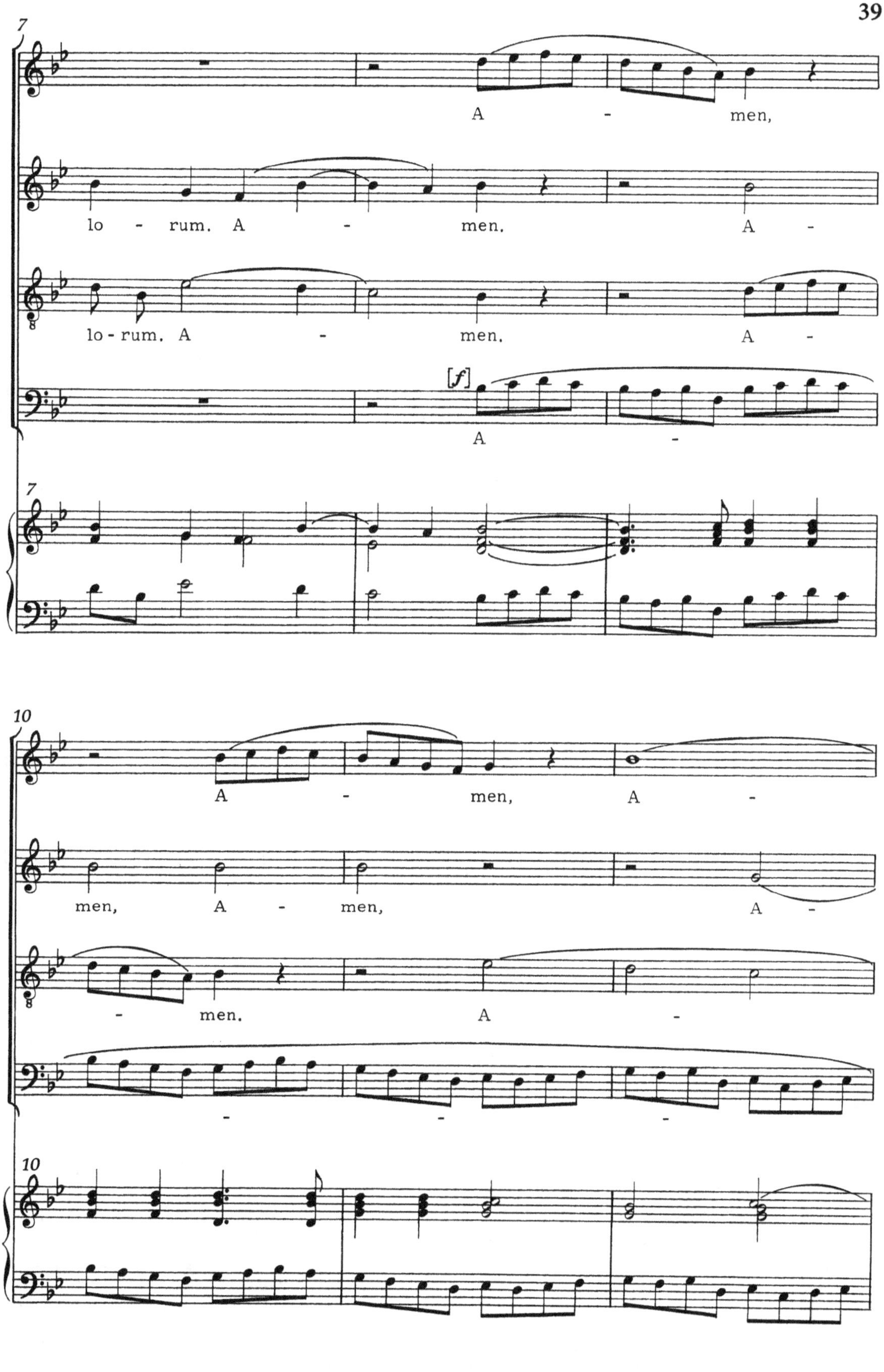
7
A - men,
lo - rum. A - men. A -
lo-rum. A - men. A -
[f]
A -
7
10
A - men, A -
men, A - men, A -
- men. A -
- - -
10

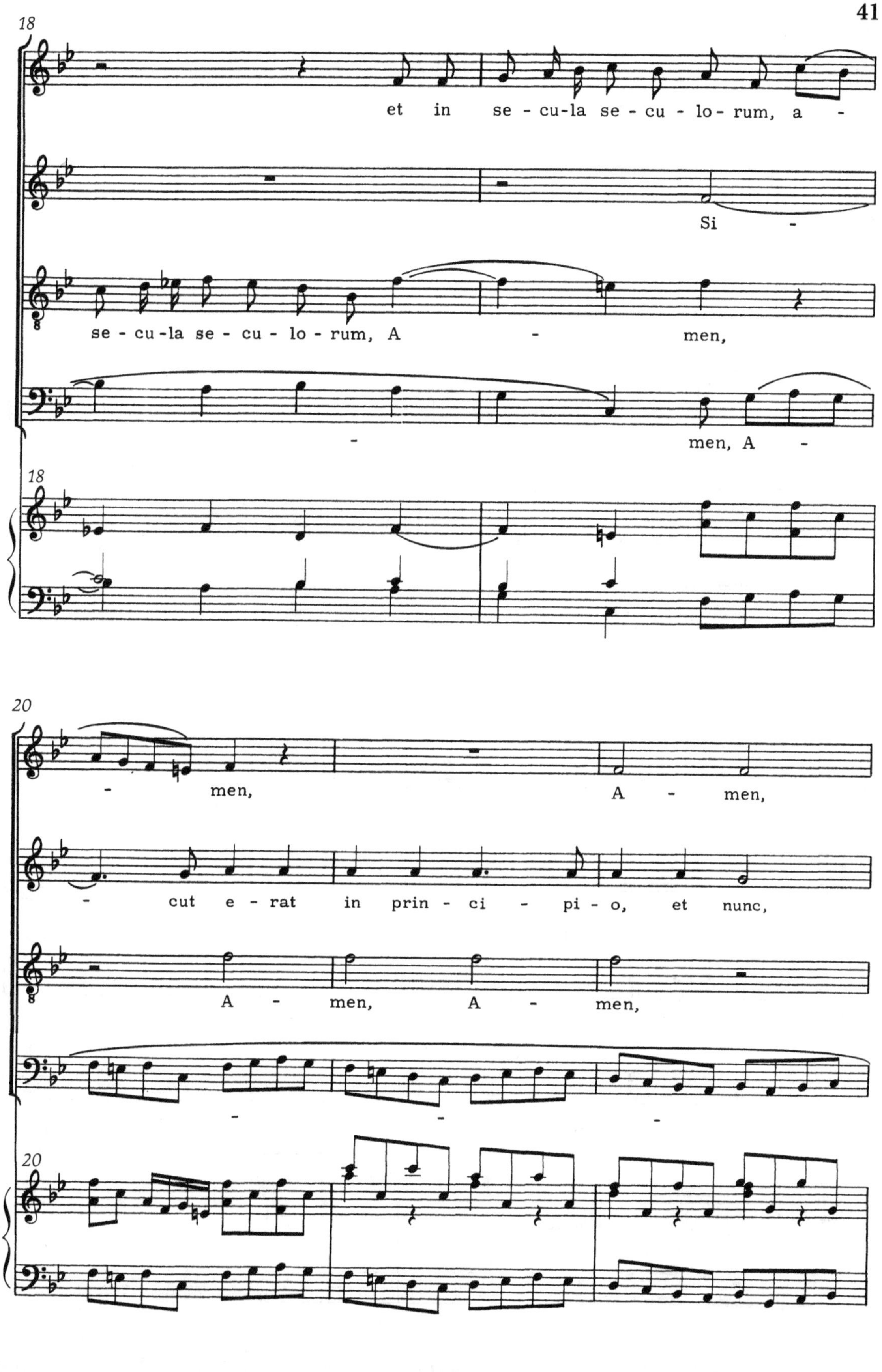
18
et in se - cu-la se - cu - lo - rum, a -
Si -
se - cu - la se - cu - lo - rum, A - men,
- men, A -
18
20
- men, A - men,
- cut e - rat in prin - ci - pi - o, et nunc,
A - men, A - men,
20

43
et in se - cu - la se - cu -
et in se - cu - la se - cu -
- men, A -
- men, A -
43
45
lo - rum, A - men,
lo - rum, A - men,
men, et in
men, et in se - cu - la se - cu - lo - rum, A -
45

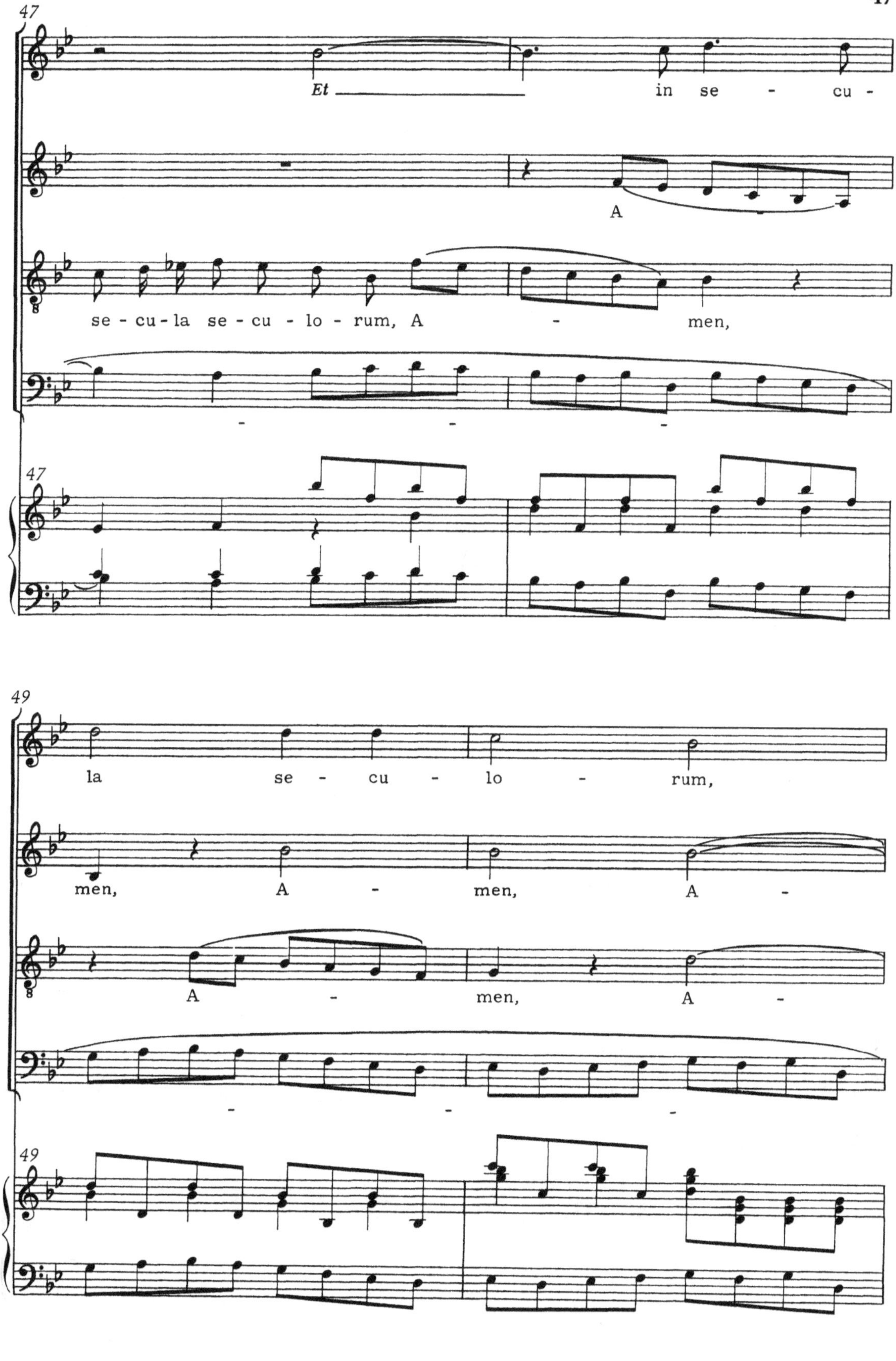
47
Et in se - cu -
A
se - cu - la se - cu - lo - rum, A - men,
47
49
la se - cu - lo - rum,
men, A - men, A -
A - men, A -
49

51
A - men, A -
- men,
- men, A -
- men,
51
53
- men, A - men, A - men.
A - men, A - men, A - men.
- men, A - men, A - men.
A - men, A - men, A - men.
53

AFTERWORD

The source for Clayton Westermann's 1968 edition of Francesco Durante's *Magnificat in B-flat major* is a manuscript copy of a score found in the Biblioteca Civica di Bergamo (I-BGc, E.1.10, f.51-74) copied in the first decade of the 19th century by Johann Simon Mayr (1763-1845). The score is inscribed: *Magnificat a 4o del Sign. Giov. Battista Pergolesi*. The widespead mistaken attribution of this work to Pergolesi arose from a 1910 monograph by Italian musicologist Giuseppe Radiciotti and propagated in the 1942 edition of Pergolesi's works prepared by Filippo Cafarelli. Radiciotti based his attribution on the above Bergamo manuscript (a copy) despite the existence of 21 other manuscript copies and two printed editions crediting the work to Pergolesi's teacher Durante. In 1982, a manuscript in Durante's own hand was discovered in Naples (Biblioteco del Conservatorio, Rari 1.6.19) for another version of the present work scored for five-part (SSATB) chorus.

As Westermann noted in his preface, Durante's score marks a skillful blending of the emerging "galant" style being adopted by the Neapolitan School and the older polyphonic style of Baroque church music. The notation of the Mayr's manuscript has been maintained in Westermann's edition except in those places where present-day notational customs serve to facilitate a practical performance. Accordingly, note values have been halved in the first and third movements; key signatures have been modified to accommodate sections which originally employed repeated use of accidentals. The original soprano, alto, and tenor clefs have been replaced by treble clefs. Slurs have been added and the flag treatment adjusted to better align with the text. The editor's English translation, placed beneath the Latin in the 1968 printing, has been removed in light of contemporary practice.

Westermann's editorial suggestions with respect to tempo and dynamics appear in brackets and recommended only in places where none existed in the source. Suggested ornaments are likewise bracketed and only prescribed at melodic or cadence points where Baroque musicians would normally apply them without indications. The performing style of the time allowed considerable freedom in ornamentation at the discretion of the performer. The indications at salient points in this edition should serve as a point of departure to an imaginative rendition. Rhythmic alterations in wide practice at the time have been noted in the fouth movement.

Durante's orchestra consists of strings and continuo (violoncello, bass, optional bassoon, and keyboard instrument - typically organ in this context). The viola part was widely sketched and for the most part simply marked "col Bassi." The continuo line abruptly skips awkwardly in places to play an octave lower than the bass voice, which led Westermann to speculate if whether a bass viol (doubling at the octave) was used in the original. Durante's five-voice setting (of which Westermann was unaware in 1968) is now thought to be a revision of the present one (for 4 voices) and the music itself differs considerably in many places. Its autograph can be consulted in detail on IMSLP, where a PDF can be downloaded and viewed.

Karel Torvik
August, 2024

www.ingramcontent.com/pod-product-compliance
Lightning Source LLC
Chambersburg PA
CBHW081023040426
42444CB00014B/3328